FOCUS ON GEOGRAPHY

Focus on Haiti

Ellen Rodger

I0805674

Crabtree Classroom
crabtreebooks.com

Crabtree Publishing

crabtreebooks.com 800-387-7650

In Canada: We acknowledge the financial support of the Government of Canada through the Canada Book Fund for our publishing activities.

Published in Canada
Crabtree Publishing
616 Welland Avenue
St. Catharines, Ontario
L2M 5V6

Published in the United States
Crabtree Publishing
347 Fifth Avenue
Suite 1402-145
New York, NY 10016

Author: Ellen Rodger
Series research and development:
Janine Deschenes
Editorial director: Kathy Middleton
Editor: Janine Deschenes
Proofreader: Roseann Biederman
Design: Tammy McGarr
Production manager: Candice Campbell
Prepress technician: Katherine Kantor

Hardcover: 978-1-0396-6122-6
Paperback: 978-1-0396-6374-9
Ebook (pdf): 978-1-0396-6817-1
Epub: 978-1-0396-8557-4
Read-along: 978-1-0396-8606-9
Audio book: 978-1-0396-6866-9

Printed in the U.S.A./CP072026

Library and Archives Canada Cataloguing in Publication Available at Library and Archives Canada

Library of Congress Cataloging-in-Publication Data
Available at the Library of Congress

Image Credits:

PIXNIO
Kendra Helmer, USAID: title page

Alamy
REUTERS / Alamy Stock Photo: p. 4, p. 25 (top), Tommy E Trenchard / Alamy Stock Photo p. 8-9 (top), M. Timothy O'Keefe / Alamy Stock Photo: p. 32, agefotostock / Alamy Stock Photo: p. 41 (bottom)

Creative Commons
Ron Knight: p. 8, Alex Carroll: p. 11, Tschoder: p 14, Jlanghurst: p. 15 (top), Stephen Malagodi: p. 39 (top), p. 39 (left center), Georges Seguin: p. 39 (bottom left), p. 39 (bottom right), Photo: Harry Wad: p. 40 (top right), Bmcao2: p. 40 (center right), Erwin509: p. 40 (bottom left), HOPE Art: front cover (top right), p. 42 (right), USAID's Bureau for Humanitarian Assistance: p. 44 (top), Jd leroy: p. 44 (bottom)

iStock
1001nights: front cover (top center), duncan1890: p. 20 (bottom), vichinterlang: p. 25 (bottom), Robert Ford: p. 34 (top right)

Library of Congress
Detroit Publishing Company photograph collection: p. 18 (bottom), p. 20 (top)

Public Domain
p. 9 (bottom), p 10 (top), Nilfanion: p. 16, Agostino Brunyen: p. 24, p. 26 (top), p. 28 (bottom right), p. 29, p. 38 (top)

Shutterstock
arindambanerjee: p. 5 (bottom), Pierre Jean Durieu: p. 6 (top), arindambanerjee: p. 17 (top left and right), Nesie Bird: p. 17 (bottom), Daniel-Alvarez: p. 18 (top), Everett Collection: p. 23 (bottom), p. 31, Ursula Page: p. 30, mikeledray: p. 35 (top), NAN728: p. 35 (bottom), Sandra Foyt: p. 36 (top), Jennifer Conway: p. 37 (top left), Daniel-Alvarez: p. 37 (top right), p. 38 (bottom), Michelle D. Milliman: p. 37 (bottom right), glenda: front cover (top left), p. 43 (top)

Wikimedia Commons
National Archives and Records Administration: p. 45

All other images from Shutterstock

Contents

INTRODUCTION

A Snapshot of Haiti

Every day, thousands of people travel from their homes in Haiti's capital, Port-au-Prince, to their factory jobs in an **industrial park** near the international airport. These women and men who work in Haiti's garment industry rise early in the morning. Many catch crowded tap taps—the colorful vans and trucks that serve as unofficial **public transport** in the country. Once at work, they spend hours cutting fabric, sewing, or packing cotton t-shirts and underwear. These are shipped and sold in North American chain retail stores.

The daily minimum wage for a worker in this kind of industry is 420 Haitian gourdes ($5.07 U.S. dollars). It isn't enough to cover full living expenses. But it is a job in a country where regular paid work is hard to find for the average person. Just 13 percent of Haiti's workforce has steady work. This leaves a lot of people in Haiti working in the **informal economy**. They sell food or goods on the street, or pick up day jobs. Most of them make $2 a day.

Other products made in Haiti's industrial parks include electronic equipment, cardboard materials, and wigs.

Revolutionary Spirit

Haiti is a small Caribbean country. It is unlike any other nation on Earth. The country was founded through a long and bloody **revolution** that freed it from **colonial** rule in the late 1700s. It became the first and only Black ruled **republic**, established by formerly enslaved people. Haiti was also the first nation to permanently ban slavery. Reminders of the revolution are everywhere in the country, from monuments to street names and murals. Generations of Haitians paid a steep price for freeing themselves. The world abandoned them and actively worked to weaken Haitian freedom. For over 200 years, Haitians have had to rely on their own skills and **ingenuity** for survival. Yet the revolutionary spirit and commitment to freedom is still strong in Haiti's people today.

A tap tap is a type of **informal transport**.

The inside of this tap tap features the word *libète* painted inside. It is the **Kreyol**, or Creole, word for freedom.

By Any Other Name

Quisqueya, Bohio, Cipango, Santo Domingo, Saint-Domingue, Ayiti. The land of Haiti has had many names, depending on who lived there, where, and when. Originally home to the **Indigenous** Taino people, it was claimed by Spain in 1492. It was later controlled by France, beginning in 1660. For 200 years, it was France's wealthiest colony. This wealth was made from the hard labor of people from Africa who were kidnapped and enslaved. In 1791, Haiti shook the world. Its enslaved people revolted, vowing to live free or die. They joined with others seeking liberty, killed their enslavers, burned their plantations, and launched more than 12 years of revolution. The revolution ended in 1804 when the new Republic of Haiti was proclaimed.

Haiti's People

Haiti's history is present in its land and all of its people. About 95 percent of Haitians are Afro-Haitian. They trace their ancestry to the enslaved peoples who were brought to the island from western Africa. About 5 percent have mixed African and European ancestry or European ancestry. Most of these people are the descendants of enslaved African women and white planters. Some are the descendants of white European soldiers who fought for Haiti's revolutionary side. A small number are the descendants of French colonists who survived the revolution, or white Europeans who settled later as merchants and traders.

Toussaint Louverture is the most well known leader of Haiti's revolution. Haiti's international airport is named after him.

AT A GLANCE

- **OFFICIAL NAME:** Republic of Haiti
- **NATIONAL CAPITAL:** Port-au-Prince
- **POPULATION:** 11,263,077
- **OFFICIAL LANGUAGES:** French, Creole
- **LAND AREA:** 10,714 square miles (27,750 sq. km)

Hispaniola lies in the Atlantic Ocean, 50 miles (80 km) east of Cuba. The Caribbean Sea is on its south coast. Haiti is located on the western third of the island. It is surrounded by ocean on three sides.

Haitian Diaspora

Haiti's first **constitution** recognized all citizens as equal and referred to all as Black. This was the revolutionary founders' attempt to avoid **prejudice**. The law of Haiti also considers people born of either a Haitian mother or father as citizens—no matter where in the world they were born. As a result, Haitian community ties are deep throughout the world. The Haitian **diaspora** is the scattering of Haitians in foreign countries. Over 2 million Haitians and people of Haitian descent live outside of Haiti. Of that number, 600,000 live in the United States, 500,000 to 800,000 in the Dominican Republic, and 165,000 in Canada. More than 100,000 also live in France and in other nations, including Caribbean islands. The diaspora has both enriched those countries and allowed Haitians abroad to support family back in Haiti.

CHAPTER 1

The Land

Mother of All Lands

Haiti shares an island with another country—the Dominican Republic. Today, the island is known as Hispaniola. Its original inhabitants, the Taino people, called it *Quisqueya*. Quisqueya is believed to mean "mother of all lands." Haiti, or Ayiti, means "mountainous land" in the Taino language.

Haiti has several mountain ranges in its north, central, and southern regions. They dip into **fertile** valleys, through grassy plains called savannas, and onto offshore islands. Haiti is snaked by rivers and streams that provide water for agriculture and drinking. It also has several freshwater and saltwater lakes.

Salty Ecosystem

Lake Azuéi is Haiti's largest lake. Located 14 miles (22 km) east of the country's capital city, Port-au-Prince, it borders the Dominican Republic. It is also known as Étang Saumâtre because it is brackish, or slightly salty. Lake Azuéi is home to 100 waterfowl species as well as American crocodiles. It forms a freshwater-to-saltwater ecosystem with Trou Caimen, another nearby salt lake, and the Enriquillo wetlands of the Dominican Republic. Mangroves, a type of tree with sturdy roots, grow on the coastal saltwater shores on the northeastern side. They are spawning grounds for fish, and feeding areas for migratory birds. There is a small, local fishing industry on the lakes as well.

The Hispaniolan Trogan is Haiti's national bird. This turquoise and grey bird is only found on the island of Hispaniola. It is among several birds that have suffered from habitat loss as forests are destroyed.

The Artibonite River extends for 199 miles (321 km). It is the longest in Haiti and forms part of the border between Haiti and the Dominican Republic. The river's waters enrich the Artibonite Plane, an area of farmland.

Mountain Ranges

About two-thirds of Haiti's land is mountainous, or above 1,600 feet (490 m). These aren't giant mountains, but they do define the rugged interior terrain. Four major mountain ranges extend west to east through Haiti to the Dominican Republic. The most northern range, the Cordillera Septentrional, runs off the northern coast of Tortue Island. This island of 70 square miles (180 square km) is also called Tortuga. It was known as a pirate island in the 1600s.

Rivers Run Through

Massif du Nord is a range of mountains that cuts through the center of the country. It is surrounded by two smaller mountain ranges to the west and south called the Cahos and the Noires mountains. The Artibonite River runs from its source in the Dominican Republic through the Massif du Nord. Its tributaries, or smaller rivers and streams, flow to the east and south through the Central Plateau. The Artibonite flows through to the Gulf of Gonave on the Caribbean Sea.

Lake Péligre is a freshwater lake and the second largest in Haiti. It was created in 1957 when a dam was built on the Artibonite River.

Closer Look

Citadelle Henri Christophe

Henri Christophe

An old fortress, built by a man who made himself King of Haiti, sits at the top of Mount Bonnet à L'Evêque, in northern Haiti. Citadelle Laferrière, or Citadelle Henri Christophe, took 15 years to construct (1805-1820). It is an example of African-style architecture in a country that fought off its plantation owners and enslavers. The Citadelle was constructed by over 20,000 formerly enslaved and self-freed Haitians. They used a mix of quick lime, molasses, animal blood, and hooves to make a strong glue for the stones. The grand fortress was intended to ward off invaders from France who wanted to take the island back after Haiti's revolution. But the man who ordered it built, Henri Christophe, died before it was put to use. Christophe was a leader of the Haitian Revolution. He created his own kingdom in northern Haiti in 1811. The Citadelle sits five miles (8 km) from the Palace of Sans-Souci, another impressive building in the mountains that Christophe had built as his home.

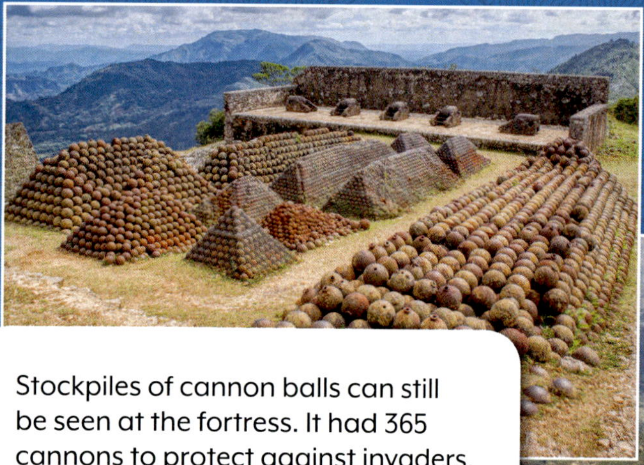

Stockpiles of cannon balls can still be seen at the fortress. It had 365 cannons to protect against invaders.

In 1982, La Citadelle was made a world heritage site by the United Nations Educational, Scientific, and Culture Organization (UNESCO). It has withstood several earthquakes without major damage.

Matheaux and Trou d'Eau Mountains

The shared mountain ranges that run through the Dominican Republic and Haiti have different names. This is because of the different languages spoken in the two countries. The French-named Matheaux and Trou d'Eau Mountains in Haiti are known as the Sierra de Neiba in Spanish-speaking Dominican Republic. These mountains are the third major range on the island. They are found in the center-west of Haiti.

Massif de la Selle

Another major mountain range in Haiti, the Massif de la Selle, reaches 8,773 feet (2,674 m). Mount Selle is the highest point in the country. Tall pine trees grow there. They are the remains of original forest that were not cut down over Haiti's history. La Selle is Haiti's first biosphere reserve. These are ecosystems that have been recognized by UNESCO as important "living laboratories." Scientists study them for their diversity of plant and animal life. To the west, the Massif de la Hotte runs into the Cayes Plain. Together with the de la Selle, these two ranges form a southern peninsula on the island. They are home to many dozens of native plant and animal species. Both ranges have a wide variety of landscapes and forests as well. They include rainforests, hardwood forests, and high-altitude dry forests.

The mountains in Haiti are mainly limestone. Many caves and subterranean, or underground, rivers run through the mountainous areas.

Port-au-Prince

Haiti's cities are located on or near its coastline. The country's capital, Port-au-Prince, is one of the oldest cities in the **Western Hemisphere**. Its colonial beginnings trace back to 1749. Located on the natural harbor of the Gulf of Gonâve on Haiti's southwest coast, it occupies 14 square miles (36 sq. km) and is home to 2.8 million people. Port-au-Prince is part of a larger **metropolitan** area that includes seven **communes**. Each are cities themselves. They include suburbs such as Pétion-Ville. There, Haiti's leaders and more wealthy residents live in gated homes or communities. Others, such as Cité Soleil, or Sun City, are home to those displaced by the harm done by poverty and natural disasters. Cité Soleil is a crowded 8 sq. miles (21 sq km) of homes and informal settlements. Around 200,000 to 500,000 people live there.

Informal settlements are groups of houses, often crowded and makeshift, that are constructed on public land. People living in informal settlements are often forced there due to a lack of affordable housing or after losing their homes in events such as natural disasters.

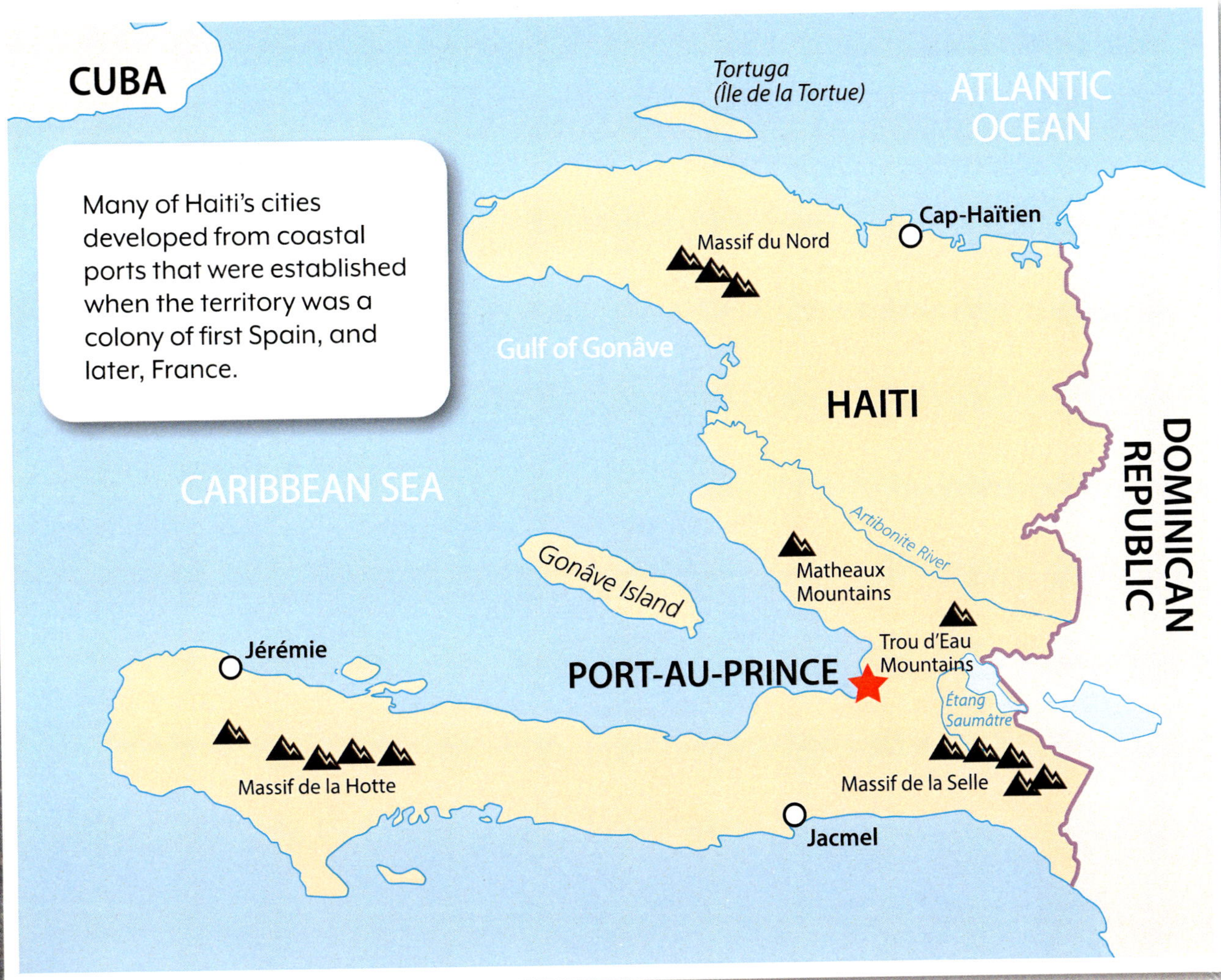

Many of Haiti's cities developed from coastal ports that were established when the territory was a colony of first Spain, and later, France.

Cap-Haïtien and Other Cities

The city of Cap-Haïtien was the largest town on the island of Hispaniola during the colonial era. Known by its nickname, Au-Cap, it is a financial and **commercial** center and, today, Haiti's second-largest city. Before the colonial era, Cap-Haïtien was a Taino village known as Guarico. The French built the city of Cap-Haïtien in 1670. It was made the capital of the colony of Saint-Domingue.

Jérémie, a small city on the northwest coast, is known as the city of poets. Many writers and poets were born there. Jérémie was also home to a Jewish community established in the 1600s. However, the community later had to move or hide their identities. Archeologists uncovered an old synagogue there in the early 2000s.

Jacmel, a commune on Haiti's southern coast, began as a Spanish colonial settlement in 1504. It was then colonized by the French in 1698. It became known as the "city of light" because of its status as the first Caribbean city to have electricity in 1925. Today, it has a population of 138,000 people.

Sun and Rain

Haiti's climate is warm and tropical. Temperatures vary by location and season. In July and August, the coastal capital of Port-au-Prince has average daily temperatures around 80 °Fahrenheit (26 °C). In January or February, highland areas can be a cool 60 °Fahrenheit (16 °C). Some areas of the country have two rainy seasons, April to June and August to November. The country's location on the **leeward** side of Hispaniola means that it gets fewer **trade winds** than its neighbor, the Dominican Republic.

Climate and Drought

Global warming and sea surface temperatures also influence Haiti's climate. This creates more fuel for hurricanes and tropical storms. The El Niño climate pattern that occurs in two- to seven-year intervals also affects Haiti. El Niño means less rain and often drought for areas of Haiti. In 2016, El Niño worsened three years of drought in the country. It withered crops that Haitians relied on to feed themselves. This created more hunger and **malnutrition**. Around 3.6 million Haitians faced **food insecurity**.

To combat climate change, Haiti has committed to planting 339,770 acres (137,500 hectares) of new forest in its 2015–2030 climate plan. It has also agreed to shift to generating renewable electricity.

Forests once covered Haiti's hills and mountainsides.

Haitians today rely on the dwindling forests for creating charcoal, which is the country's main cooking fuel.

Forestry and Farming

Before Haiti was colonized, rich forests covered its land. Spanish and French planters began cutting huge areas of the cedar, pine, and juniper forests for cattle ranges and sugar cane, coffee, and **indigo** plantations. For 200 years, more and more forest was sacrificed to increase plantation profits. After colonization ended, the new country of Haiti was forced to cut valuable mahogany trees to pay debts forced upon it. Today, few of the original forests remain. Without trees and forests as anchors, the soil washes away during heavy rains.

One recent study estimates that Haiti's primary, or uncut and replanted, forests will disappear by 2036. Several animal species are expected to become extinct along with the forests.

Hurricane Belt

Haiti is located right in the middle of the hurricane belt, or "alley." Severe storms and hurricanes batter the island of Hispaniola in hurricane season, between June and November. Hurricane season can mean a half dozen or more hurricanes of varying strength hit Haiti in a six-month period. Hurricanes can kill thousands and cause major flooding and damage to crops and homes. In 1963, Hurricane Flora killed over 8,000 Haitians.

Storm Devastation

In 2016, Hurricane Matthew struck southwestern Haiti. It destroyed 90 percent of the houses along the southern coast. It also washed away important infrastructure such as bridges and medical clinics. An estimated 546 people were killed, but the numbers are believed to be higher. Natural disasters mean Haiti must request help from other countries to help feed people, provide safe drinking water, and set up temporary housing.

A Fault Runs Through It

The island of Hispaniola sits on the border of the North American and Caribbean **tectonic plates**. A series of interconnected **fault lines** run through the plates. Two of the major fault lines run through Haiti in the north and south. When tension builds up at the faults, it is released as energy as the plates slide across each other. The energy is known as an earthquake. Haiti had major earthquakes in 1751 and 1770 that collapsed buildings and destroyed towns. Earthquakes have continued to cause devastation in the country today.

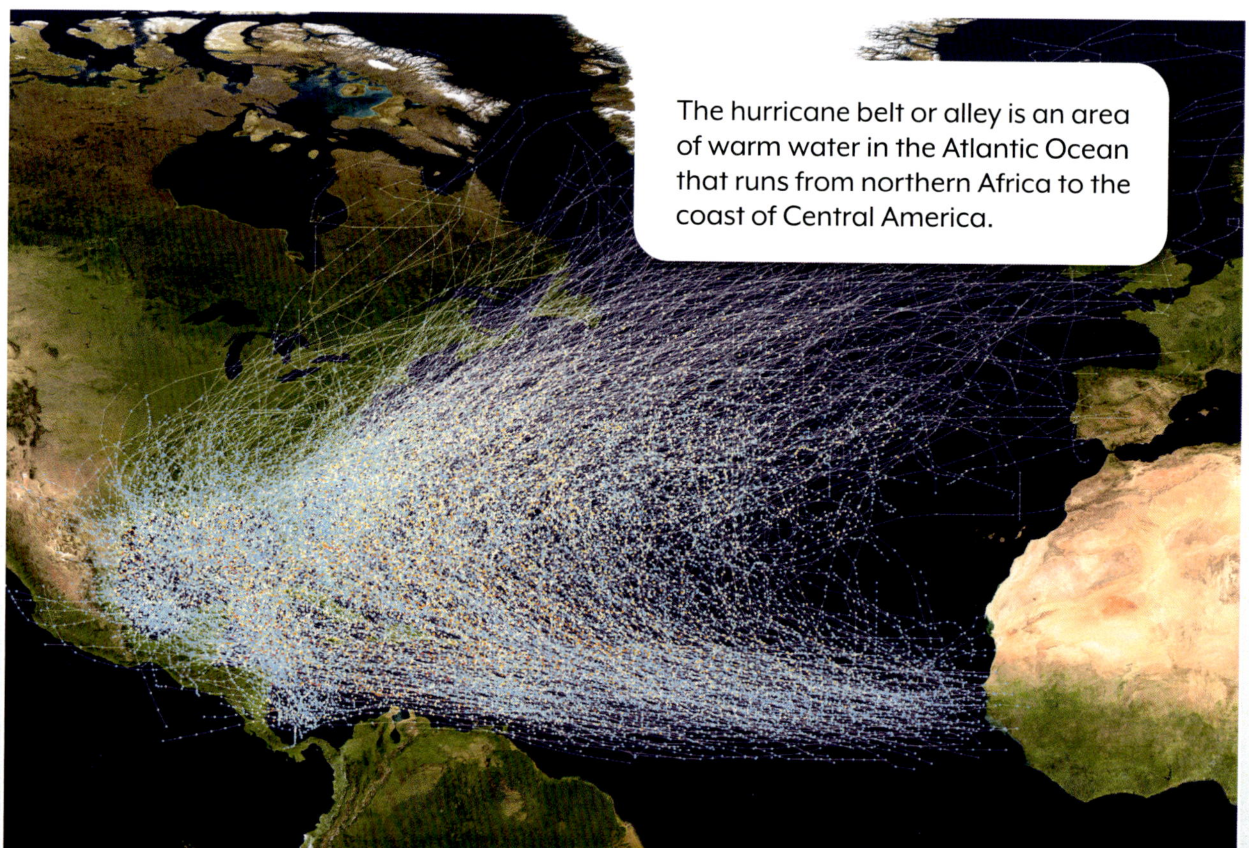

The hurricane belt or alley is an area of warm water in the Atlantic Ocean that runs from northern Africa to the coast of Central America.

This tent camp was constructed for earthquake survivors who lost their homes.

Closer Look

In the weeks and months that followed the earthquake, outbreaks of cholera killed thousands more people.

The 2010 Earthquake

Haitians were shopping for food at markets, sitting down for meetings, or making their way home from work. Children were playing in their granmé's kitchens. And then it hit. On January 12, 2010, at 4:53 p.m., the ground shook and rumbled. Buildings collapsed, and entire sections of cities were leveled to the ground. People were trapped under the rubble. The 7.0 magnitude earthquake located 15 miles (24 km) from Port-au-Prince was followed by several aftershocks in the moments and days that followed. The country was devastated. Over 300,000 people died. Thousands more were injured and one million were left homeless.

Haiti was unable to prepare for a disaster like this. There were no earthquake-resistant buildings and the country had inadequate clean water supplies and electricity. The Port-au-Prince cathedral, United Nations headquarters, national penitentiary, and parliament were partly destroyed. The earthquake recovery was slow and took years. Many people lived in tent camps for months. They survived on international relief and help from family. In 2017, the United Nations estimated about 55,000 people were still displaced and living in camps. On August 14, 2021, a 7.2 magnitude earthquake struck Haiti's southern coast. An estimated 2,000 people were killed. The city of Les Cayes was hard hit, with over 37,000 homes destroyed and many more damaged.

Haiti's National Palace was among the important buildings badly damaged by the 2010 earthquake.

CHAPTER 2

Becoming Haiti

The Taino were the original inhabitants of Haiti and the island of Hispaniola. They were an Indigenous people whose roots and language can be traced to South America. Taino settlements were spread throughout the Caribbean around 400 B.C. Archeologists think the Taino population on Hispaniola may have been from one to three million at the time Spain reached Haiti in 1492.

Some of what is known about the Taino comes from what Spanish explorers wrote. Some comes from later historians who have pieced together and interpreted history from **cultural artifacts**. Most stories are incomplete and miss the Taino people's perspective. We know from records kept by the Spanish that contact with Europeans destroyed the Taino. Historians believe most died during warfare or of harsh treatment after being enslaved by the Spanish and forced to work on early plantations and in mines. Some also died of diseases carried by Europeans. New research shows many Taino intermarried with Spanish, and later French and Africans. Today, some Haitians claim Taino ancestry.

Spanish records show that a smallpox **epidemic** in Hispaniola in 1518-1519 killed almost 90 percent of the surviving Taino.

At least one modern study has shown many Caribbean island residents have Taino **DNA**.

Taino Culture

The Taino used caves on the island of Hispaniola for more than 1,000 years before the Spanish came. Their shamans, or religious leaders, performed ceremonies there. Spanish historical documents said the Taino communities included larger cities and smaller settlements called *yucayeques*. Their homes were *bohios*, or circular buildings made from wooden poles, straw, and palm leaves. Taino women farmed crops such as cassava, corn, beans, and tobacco. Men fished and hunted using canoes made from hollowed trees. They also traded with other Taino peoples throughout the Caribbean. Several *caciques*, or chiefs, ruled the island. Chiefs were advised by healers and "nobles" who ruled over others. After European contact, Taino culture and knowledge was passed on to the island's Spanish, African, and French inhabitants.

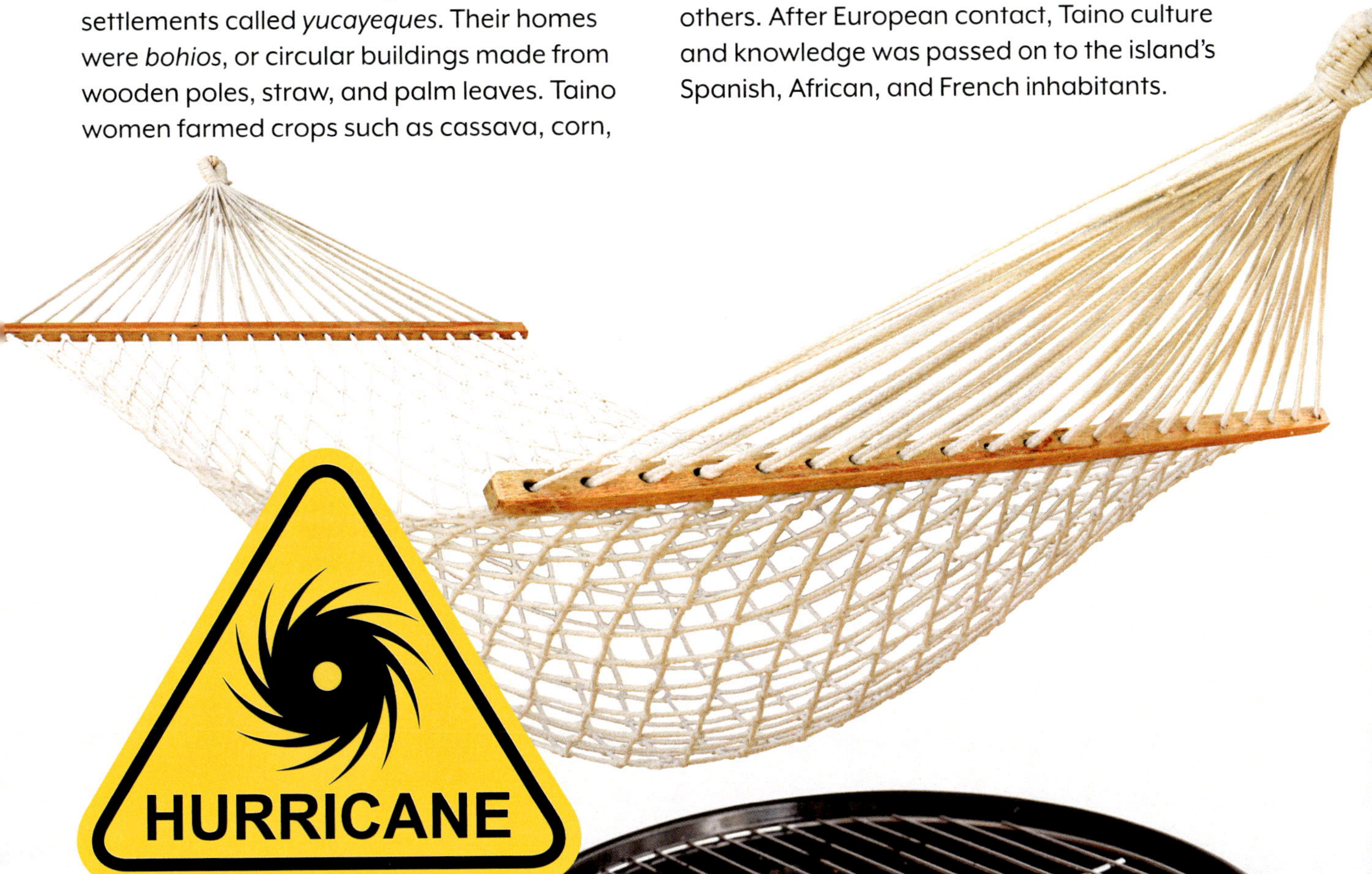

Parts of Taino language and culture survive today and are used by people all over the world, including the words hurricane, *hamaca*, or hammock, and *barbacoa*, or barbecue.

Spanish Rule

Santa Maria

Italian explorer Christopher Columbus claimed the island of *La Española*—later called Hispaniola—for Spain on December 5, 1492. Columbus was searching for a western sea route to the trade riches of Asia. One of his three ships, the Santa Maria, sank off the coast on Christmas Eve 1492. A Taino cacique named Guacanagari allowed the Spaniards to leave 39 men behind at a settlement in present-day northeastern Haiti. Relations were good at first. However, the Taino later killed the Spanish men after they threatened Taino women.

Columbus returned to La Española in 1493, and again in 1498. He brought Spanish settlers for a new colony farther to the east at Santo Domingo, in what is now the Dominican Republic side of the island. Columbus became governor of the new colony. He set up the encomienda system, where Taino were forced to work for the Spanish and give tribute, or payment, in return for "protection." In reality, the Taino were worked to death on plantations or in mines. Many resisted this form of enslavement and died in battles with the Spanish. Some Taino escaped enslavement and hid in the hills of the island. They emerged to launch surprise attacks against the Spanish.

La Española means "Spanish Island." Remains of colonial settlements can be found around the island, such as this old fortress in Santo Domingo, the capital of the Dominican Republic.

This engraving depicts the Taino encountering Columbus on Hispaniola in 1492.

La Española to The Main

Columbus and his family proved poor governors of the colony. The settlers revolted. Eventually, the court of the Spanish king ruled Hispaniola. From 1503 onward, Africans were brought over to replace the Taino as enslaved labor. For over 100 years, the island was a military outpost for Spain in the Americas. Hispaniola also served as a headquarters of the Spanish conquistadors. They were conquerors who set out to colonize the New World. Hernando Cortes's conquest of Mexico was launched from Santo Domingo. So was Ponce de León's colonization of Puerto Rico. But with Spain's interests focused on its new colonies in the **Spanish Main** and the wealth they brought, Hispaniola lost strength.

Closer Look

Maroon Communities

In 1522, enslaved Africans led one of the first revolts, or resistances, in North America. It occurred on the sugar plantation of Christopher Columbus's son, Diego Columbus. Many people escaped their enslavement and fled to the mountains. There, they established **Maroon** communities and joined the remaining Taino. From the mountains, they launched battles against the Spanish, and later, French colonizers.

Formerly enslaved Africans established Maroon communities in many colonies, including Jamaica and Brazil. The settlements were armed for protection against enslavers.

Spain Loses Control

By the mid-1500s, pirates from other European **empires** were terrorizing ship traffic on the Caribbean Sea. Smuggling became a way of life among Spanish colonists. To stop the smuggling, Spain forced its settlers on Hispaniola to move to Santo Domingo. This meant many people starved as their cattle were set free. Pirates took over the coast of Hispaniola and the islands nearby. The island of Tortuga became a pirate stronghold under French control by 1659. For years, the European empires fought over territories in Europe and the Americas. In 1697, Spain formally gave up the western part of Hispaniola to the French. France called its new colony Saint-Domingue.

coffee berries

cotton

French Control

From the start, France set about making Saint-Domingue profitable. Colonists set up plantations, soon making Saint-Domingue France's most wealthy colony. All of its wealth was based on export of crops grown by enslaved humans. Saint-Domingue was a horror for the Africans stolen from their homes, shipped there, and enslaved. Its enslaved people numbered 500,000 by 1789. Its white population was just 32,000.

cocoa pod

Plantations in Saint-Domingue grew sugar, coffee, cocoa, coconuts, tobacco, spices, cotton, and indigo. The colony's success meant it became known as the "pearl of the Antilles."

At its height in the mid-to-late-1700s, Saint-Domingue earned France billions in trade and tax income. The wealth came from the labor of enslaved people.

Between the 16th and 19th centuries, an estimated 10 to 12 million enslaved Africans were transported across the Atlantic to provide labor in colonies. The ships were overcrowded and conditions were brutal.

Brutal Conditions

Saint-Domingue's white planters were known for their casual cruelty. Enslavers did not consider enslaved people fully human. That meant that common methods of punishment and control included burning or burying people alive and cutting off ears or hands. The conditions were so brutal that enslaved women dreaded having children and bringing them into a life of suffering. Enslaved women were regularly assaulted and bore the children of their enslavers. These children were often freed by their fathers. They and their descendants became known as *gens de couleur libres*, or free people of color. Some male free people of color were educated by their white fathers and sent to France for schooling or military training.

Affranchis and freed people of color could own land and earn money as artisans or shopkeepers. However, they did not have the same rights as white men, such as the right to vote.

Class and Race

Race and **class** dominated colonial society in Saint-Domingue. White people were either *grands blancs* or *petits blancs*. Grands blancs owned plantations and enslaved people. Petits blancs were working people, or artisans and shopkeepers. They may have also had enslaved people working for them. There were also *affranchis*, or enslaved Black people who were legally freed by their enslavers, as well as free people of color, and enslaved people. Maroons, or self-freed Black people, lived in communities hidden in the mountains.

Language and Resistance

White enslavers might have thought they were in total control, but they could not conquer the enduring desire enslaved people had to live free. Enslaved people resisted their bondage from the very beginning. One way they resisted is through their language. They developed a new language to communicate with each other while they worked on plantations. *Kreyòl Ayisyen*, or Haitian Creole, evolved from several West African languages, as well as Spanish, French, Portuguese, and Taino.

Haitian Creole is now an official language of Haiti. It is the first language of roughly 11 million people in Haiti and around the world. Vodou is also recognized as a national religion in modern Haiti.

Religion and Liberation

Enslaved people on Saint-Domingue also developed their own religious belief system, called Vodou. It too evolved as a blend of traditional African religions. White Christian planters on Saint-Domingue didn't understand Vodou and viewed it as a threat. They tried to stop enslaved people from practicing it. The white planters were right about one thing: Vodou represented a liberation. Kreyol-speaking people who practiced Vodou were a big part of the resistance to slavery. This resistance eventually led to the end of slavery in Saint-Domingue.

Each year, believers from all over Haiti attend the Plaine du Nord festival. People worship and celebrate Vodou gods and their African heritage. The festival involves bathing in mud baths, as shown here.

Ripe for Change

By the mid-1700s, Saint-Domingue supplied most of the world's sugar. The enslaved people who planted and harvested the crops outnumbered the white planters and merchants nine to one. Many ran away to Maroon villages and launched raids on plantations. These were continually put down, but the resistance was never extinguished. The brutal conditions of life in Saint-Domingue for enslaved people and the denial of rights for free people of color led to more uprisings in the late 1700s. In 1789, the **French Revolution** overthrew the King of France. Revolutionaries there drafted the Declaration of the Rights of Man and of the Citizen. This was a document that asserted the rights of French citizens. It included the right to vote. Free people of color wanted these same rights for themselves in Saint-Domingue.

Some Black revolutionaries were skilled soldiers. Some free people of color had served in the French military. Many newly enslaved people brought to the island colony had also been skilled soldiers in Africa.

Bois Caïman

After many petitions, France's revolutionary government granted citizenship for wealthy free people of color on Saint-Domingue in 1791. But the colony's white planters rejected this. Soon, Saint-Domingue was boiling over. On the stormy night of August 14, 1791, hundreds of enslaved people attended a secret Vodou ceremony in Bois Caïman, a wooded area near Cap-Haïtien on the north coast. The ceremony was the result of months of planning by many leaders. They then returned to the plantations, burned them, and killed many of their enslavers. The revolt was the beginning of the Haitian Revolution.

The revolution, spearheaded by leaders such as Henri Christophe, spread from the northern plains to the south. It soon involved 100,000 formerly enslaved Black people.

The Haitian Revolution

The Haitian Revolution was not short or uncomplicated. For 12 years and 4 months (1791-1804), the colony was in some stage of conflict. The revolutionaries, including Saint-Domingue's free people of color, fought long and endured hardships. All were determined to live free. France was alarmed that rebels controlled its wealthy colony. It abolished slavery—after the enslaved in Saint-Domingue had freed themselves. France also granted civil and political rights to all Black men in its colonies, in 1793. But it was too late. The revolution could not be stopped.

By 1799, France was controlled by Napoleon Bonaparte. He wanted to re-establish control of the riches of Saint-Domingue and return to slavery under "better conditions." The leaders of the revolt realized that the people of Saint-Domingue could not remain free in a colony of France. One leader, Toussaint Louverture, drew up a constitution in 1801. It called for Black rule in a free and independent Black state. France sent troops to invade. For two more years, the rebels fought, defeating the French in several battles and forcing them to leave the island. On January 1, 1804, the new, independent Republic of Haiti was proclaimed.

Closer Look

Toussaint Louverture

Haiti's Revolutionary Heroes

The revolution required the support of many people from different groups and classes of Saint-Domingue society. These included enslaved Black people, free people of color, women, and even a few white foreign fighters. Some became leaders of the new Republic of Haiti. Toussaint Louverture is probably Haiti's most well-known hero and leader. The details of his early life are disputed, but it is known that he was enslaved at a young age and educated by his godfather, who was a free man. Toussaint was free by age 33 and managed a coffee plantation. He became a skilled military leader during the revolution and took control of the island in 1801. France sent troops to regain control. They tricked Louverture into meeting with them, arrested him, and shipped him to France. He died there in 1803 while imprisoned. Other rebel generals rallied and continued the revolution, finally forcing the French out in 1804.

Jean-Jacques Dessalines
Born into slavery, Dessalines rose to command armies during the revolution. He became the first leader of independent Haiti before his assassination in 1806.

Alexandre Pétion
Born a gens de couleur, Pétion was educated in France and returned to fight in the revolution. Like many rebels, he switched sides from the French to the rebels. Pétion became the first president of the Republic of Haiti in 1807 and served until his death in 1818.

Jean-Baptiste Sans Souci
Sans Souci was a rebel leader and commander of enslaved *Bossales*, or African-born people, during the revolution. He never allied with the French and was known for his guerilla-style attacks. Fearing his power, Henri Christophe (see page 10) had Sans Souci assassinated after the revolution. He then built a palace to his memory and called it Sans-Souci, which means carefree.

Sanite Bélair
Born a free Black woman in Saint-Domingue, Bélair became a lieutenant in Louverture's army. She was captured by the French during the revolution and executed along with her husband, also a soldier. Bélair is depicted on a modern Haitian banknote.

Marie-Madeleine Lachenais
Also known as Joute, she was a political advisor and partner to two Haitian presidents—Alexandre Pétion and Jean-Pierre Boyer. She helped influence laws and government.

Jean-Jacques Dessalines

Alexandre Pétion

Sanite Bélair

Marie-Madeleine Lachenais

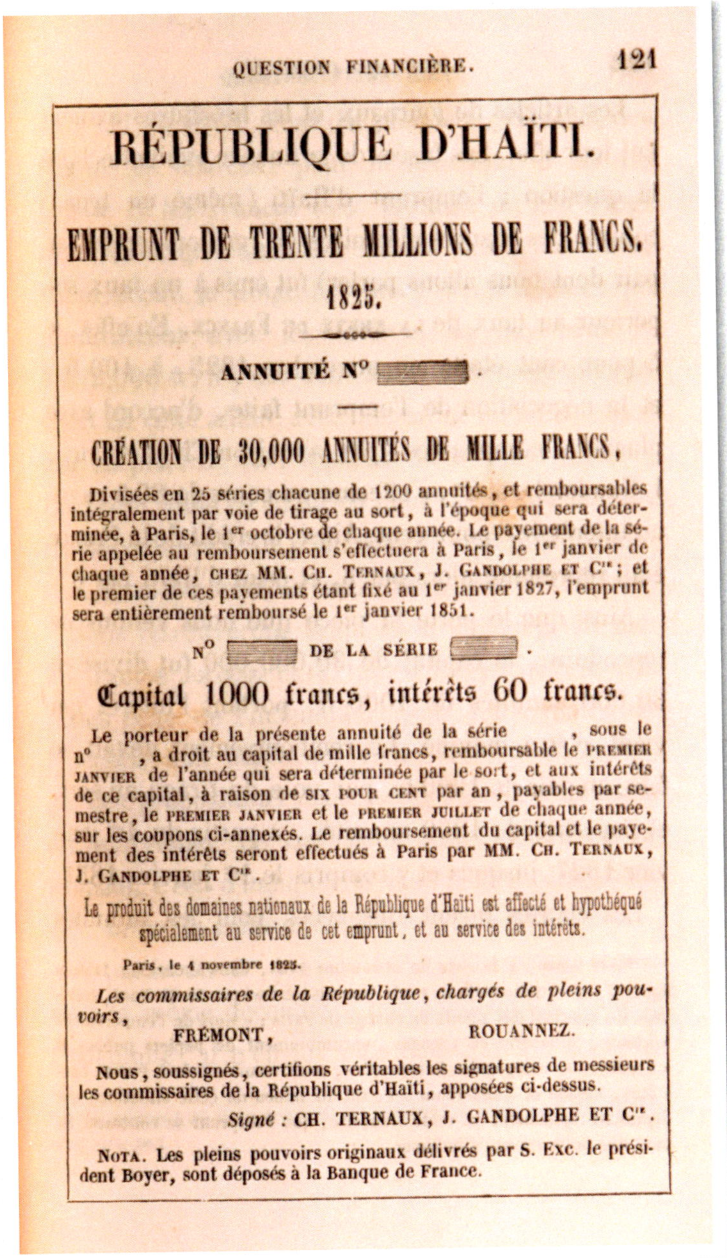
QUESTION FINANCIÈRE. 121

RÉPUBLIQUE D'HAÏTI.

EMPRUNT DE TRENTE MILLIONS DE FRANCS.

1825.

ANNUITÉ N° ▬▬ .

CRÉATION DE 30,000 ANNUITÉS DE MILLE FRANCS,

Divisées en 25 séries chacune de 1200 annuités, et remboursables intégralement par voie de tirage au sort, à l'époque qui sera déterminée, à Paris, le 1er octobre de chaque année. Le payement de la série appelée au remboursement s'effectuera à Paris, le 1er janvier de chaque année, CHEZ MM. CH. TERNAUX, J. GANDOLPHE ET Cie; et le premier de ces payements étant fixé au 1er janvier 1827, l'emprunt sera entièrement remboursé le 1er janvier 1851.

N° ▬▬ DE LA SÉRIE ▬▬ .

Capital 1000 francs, intérêts 60 francs.

Le porteur de la présente annuité de la série , sous le n° , a droit au capital de mille francs, remboursable le PREMIER JANVIER de l'année qui sera déterminée par le sort, et aux intérêts de ce capital, à raison de SIX POUR CENT par an, payables par semestre, le PREMIER JANVIER et le PREMIER JUILLET de chaque année, sur les coupons ci-annexés. Le remboursement du capital et le payement des intérêts seront effectués à Paris par MM. CH. TERNAUX, J. GANDOLPHE ET Cie.

Le produit des domaines nationaux de la République d'Haïti est affecté et hypothéqué spécialement au service de cet emprunt, et au service des intérêts.

Paris, le 4 novembre 1825.

Les commissaires de la République, chargés de pleins pouvoirs,

FRÉMONT, ROUANNEZ.

Nous, soussignés, certifions véritables les signatures de messieurs les commissaires de la République d'Haïti, apposées ci-dessus.

Signé : CH. TERNAUX, J. GANDOLPHE ET Cie.

NOTA. Les pleins pouvoirs originaux délivrés par S. Exc. le président Boyer, sont déposés à la Banque de France.

In addition to the indemnity, France also forced Haiti to give it a 50 percent discount on exports. This made the debt more difficult to pay off.

High Price of Freedom

For many generations, the people of Haiti paid a high price for their freedom. After independence, enslaver countries feared Haiti's successful revolt would inspire more enslaved people to revolt. The United States, England, Spain, and other countries refused to recognize Haiti or trade with it. They **boycotted** the new nation. Independent Haiti had no allies. It also had no way of earning the money it needed to repair and grow after years of revolution. Many years of political and economic struggle followed.

The Indemnity

In 1825, France returned with warships and threats. It demanded Haiti **compensate** plantation owners for the loss of its profitable colony and the humans they enslaved. In return, it would recognize Haiti as an independent state and encourage other countries to trade with Haiti.

Haiti's leaders were forced to agree in order to prevent a new war. The self-freed people of Haiti would pay their former enslavers 150 million francs for their own freedom and Haitian land. Haiti had to borrow the money from French banks to pay this debt, called an **indemnity**. When Haiti could not pay the loan in 1838, France reduced the debt to 90 million francs—or about $21 billion in today's dollars. Haitians finally paid the final interest payment on the debt in 1947.

Haiti in a New World

The early years of the new republic were difficult. Most of Haiti's people had never known freedom. The country's leaders struggled to govern and pay the indemnity debt. Many vied for power. Haiti's first president, Jean-Jacques Dessalines, was a hero of the revolution and fiercely dedicated to freedom. He had inspired generals to push the French out of Saint-Domingue. He made sure the country's constitution was ratified, or made official. Then, in 1804, he crowned himself Emperor Jacques I. He was later assassinated in 1806.

Soon after independence, the country was split in two. There was a republic, led by Alexandre Pétion, in the south. A kingdom, led by Henri Christophe, was established in the north. The country was reunited in 1820. However, things were still unstable with **coups** and changes in government. Despite the instability, Haiti was still a beacon of freedom for many people fighting against enslavement and colonial rule. It provided citizenship to enslaved Black people escaping from other countries. Haiti also supported anti-colonial revolutions in other countries, including Venezuela and Columbia.

The payments to France cost Haiti over a century and a half of progress. More than 80 percent of the country's wealth was used to pay the debt, preventing Haiti from building its economy.

U.S. Marines occupied Haiti for 19 years. They used forced labor to help build the country's infrastructure, such as roads.

Freedom Curtailed

In 1915, the United States invaded Haiti. It occupied the country until 1934. The invasion and occupation was said to "maintain order." But in reality, U.S. banks were concerned about Haiti's inability to pay debts owed to them. Haitians were angered by the occupation. Their complaints and uprisings were met with violence. Haiti became a U.S. **protectorate** until 1934—training a new generation of Haitian officials and leaders.

The U.S. kept financial control of Haiti until 1947. This led to more unstable rule and **dictatorships**. From 1957 to 1986, Haiti was ruled by the Duvalier family. Father and son Francois and Jean-Claude Duvalier used the country like a personal bank. They stole close to $1 billion. The Duvalier's brutal police force oppressed and murdered people who spoke out. An estimated 60,000 were killed. Others were kidnapped, never to be heard from again. Many Haitians left the country. The Duvalier regime ended in 1986, when the Haitian people rose up and Jean-Claude fled to France. In 1990, Haiti held its first free, **democratic** election in many years. But that government was overthrown by the military after eight months. More instability followed. Haiti's most recent president, Jovenel Moise, was assassinated in his home in July 2021. The assassins were a group of foreign killers hired by an opponent of Moise.

CHAPTER 3

Life Today

Daily life is difficult for the majority of Haitians today. Roughly 59 percent of the population lives below the **poverty line**. Haiti's history of colonization and crippling debt made economic and democratic growth very difficult. For many years, the government was ruled by **elites** who did not look after the interests of all. From 1986 to 2021 alone, Haiti was governed by 18 different leaders.

Despite harsh or disordered governments, however, the revolutionary spirit of the people of Haiti prevails. Its people are strong because they have to be. To survive in a world hostile to their success, they have had no other choice.

Haitian art shows the vibrant spirit of the country. It often reflects African heritage, with Indigenous and European influences. Paintings are often colorful. Popular scenes are busy markets with a lot of people.

Haiti was the world's third-largest coffee producer in 1949. However, the industry later suffered from lack of investment.

Smallholder Farming

About 65 percent of Haitians work in agriculture. They grow crops such as bananas, plantains, yams, and rice for mostly local markets. Commercial coffee farms in the mountains produce beans for local and small export markets. Small family-owned coffee farms, however, have been remaking the country's coffee industry. Many are transforming mountainsides made bare from centuries of deforestation. The Arabica coffee beans grown in Haiti's northern regions need shade-covered mountainsides. Planting trees and coffee plants helps prevent soil erosion. However, global warming is forcing many farmers to adjust and plant even higher up the mountains, where it is cooler.

Cocoa and Vetiver

Cocoa beans and mangoes are also export crops. About 20,000 **smallholder** farms grow cocoa beans as a cash crop in what Haitian farmers call "creole gardens." These are small lots where coconut, breadfruit, mango, and avocado trees shield the cocoa trees. The cocoa is sold to a growing market of specialty chocolate producers throughout the world. Haiti is also known as one of the world's major producers of vetiver. Vetiver is a tall grass plant that is used in perfumes and oils. It is grown in the Les Cayes region, in western Haiti.

Eighty percent of the world's commercially produced vetiver oil comes from Haiti. Its smoky scented oil is favored by fine perfume makers.

Soil Erosion

Soil erosion is a major problem in Haiti. The country has lost an estimated 98 percent of its forests. Much of this deforestation is due to centuries of clear cutting for plantations and farms. More recently, deforestation has been fueled by the need for cooking fuel. Charcoal is the main fuel used for cooking in Haiti. Charcoal makers strip the forests to burn the wood to make charcoal. However, there are ways charcoal makers can help save trees and the environment. They can leave tree roots to regrow after cutting, and plant beans and yams in between the roots. With these roots and plants, soil is less likely to wash away. Creating a regulated charcoal-making industry can also help prevent deforestation. It would make sure charcoal makers have work while benefiting the environment by ensuring trees are replanted.

Soil erosion is a big problem in Haiti as many people rely on farming for food and income.

Vetiver has deep roots that help stabilize the soil, preventing soil erosion. However, uprooting it when harvesting can have the opposite effect. Farmers are using new harvesting techniques to reduce this.

A small export fishing industry exists off Haiti's coasts. Its markets include the U.S., Canada, and other countries. Most Haitian fishers catch and sell to local markets, however.

Population and Environment

The urban areas of Haiti are densely populated and growing. Even with a growing population, Haiti has a low per capita, or per person, **ecological footprint**. Haitians are not mass consumers or producers of **carbon**. When controlled for population, Haiti is second in the world for the smallest ecological footprint. By comparison, Australia ranked third highest and Canada fifth highest. Larger economies consume more than they replace. Haiti has few major industries. They are focused mostly on local markets, such as cement making or sugar refining. There are some export industries such as clothing, agriculture, scrap metal, and toy manufacturing. However, it is difficult for Haiti to attract and maintain many industries. This is due to its instability and lack of infrastructure, such as paved roads.

Tourism is a source of income in Haiti, but it is small compared to its neighbor, the Dominican Republic. Some cruise ship companies have leased land and built ports such as Labadee, in northern Haiti. These provide income for some Haitians, but nothing is secure.

Infrastructure and Aid

Up to 75 percent of Haitians are unemployed or underemployed and working part time jobs. Many who are employed earn wages that do not meet their needs. The better jobs are in government services, tourism, and organizations that provide **foreign aid** in the country. It is difficult for Haiti to grow its industries without good roads, proper water and sewage treatment, regular electricity, and reliable Internet. In addition, the institutions that ensure personal safety, such as the police, are not trusted by many Haitians.

The average Haitian walks a lot. Foot transportation is the most cost effective way of getting around.

Remittances

Haiti's economy is dependent on foreign aid and charitable groups. Remittances contribute more than 3.2 billion dollars a year to Haiti's economy. These are support payments from Haitians living and working in other countries to family and friends in Haiti. Natural disasters mean even more aid and support are needed. For example, the 2010 earthquake caused an estimated $7.8 billion in damages. This figure is 120 percent of Haiti's **gross domestic product**.

Many aid groups and foreign governments promise to "build back better." The Haitian people don't always trust this. They have seen invasions and **interventions** in their country before. Some have destroyed markets. Other times, aid money went to leaders who were not accountable to the people.

Haitians abroad also contribute to their homeland's economy by buying Haitian-made products, such as foods from home, and by setting up or supporting Haitian businesses.

Closer Look

While wealthier people and the middle class live in gated communities with modern amenities, most people live in small houses with no running water. These are the neighborhoods in which gangs operate.

The UN mission in Haiti is criticized for abuses, such as sexual assault and violence, carried out by peacekeepers against Haitian civilians.

Gangs of Haiti

When the world has intervened, things often haven't gone well. For over a decade (2004-2017) a UN peacekeeping force was in Haiti. It aimed to keep armed gangs under control and to prevent the Haitian National Police from committing **atrocities**. However, many Haitians saw it as a force of occupation—much like the U.S. Marines were, a century earlier. The country's gangs control entire cities or communes. Some are made up of former soldiers and police officers. Politicians and business elites are believed to associate with gangs to protect their positions and businesses. Gang kidnappings happen regularly, and local journalists and human rights activists have been killed for speaking out. The gangs operate in neighborhoods where the government provides little or no services. In some places, the gangs are the services. They distribute food rations provided by charities. They feed students and pay them to do jobs. When the students leave school, they join the gangs as there is nothing else for them to do.

Education is limited to grade school for many people. Schools are overcrowded. Children are educated in French, but most of the population speaks Creole.

A Vibrant Country

"*Piti Piti Zwazo Fe Nic Li*" is a Kreyol proverb or saying. In English, it translates to "little by little the bird builds his nest." It can apply to many things in Haiti, from how the country was formed, to how Haitians developed their own culture and ways of life. The Kreyol language was developed little by little over hundreds of years. Kreyol is integral to Haitian music, dance, and the Haitian-born religion of Vodou. Haitian writers have built their own body of books and poems in their native tongue. The country's national anthem, *La Dessalinienne*, even has separate lyrics in French and Kreyol. The Kreyol version was written many years later. It reflects the pride Haitians have in the blood that was shed for freedom.

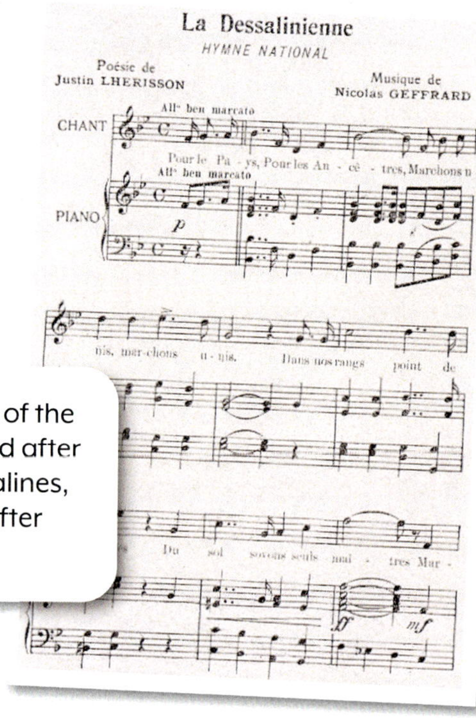

The French version of the anthem was named after Jean-Jacques Dessalines, Haiti's first leader after the revolution.

Going to School

About 80 percent of schools in Haiti are privately run by religious organizations, non-profits, or for-profit groups. These schools charge tuition. This means some families cannot afford to send their children every year. As a result, many Haitians need extra years to finish school. Schools have increased enrollments by participating in tuition waiver programs. In school, Haitian children learn in Kreyol for the first three years. After that, they study mostly in French. The national exams students must complete to graduate are in French. There is a push to make Kreyol the language of instruction throughout schools. It would help students to learn better if they were taught in their own language, which is spoken by 90 to 95 percent of Haitians. Haiti also has several universities and schools of higher education, including the Université d'Etat d'Haiti, or National University of Haiti.

A group of Haitian students protest for improvements to education, such as increased funding for public school.

Closer Look

Felix Morriseau-Leroy, or "Moriso"

Haiti's Language

The grammar and sentence structure of Kreyol is related to the Gbe languages spoken by the Benin cultures of Africa. It is also infused with Taino, French, Spanish, English, and Portuguese. Kreyol is not a simple "mix." It is an artful blend that represents a sense of place. Kreyol united people from different African cultures and helped them survive on slave plantations. Different from the French language of the island's planters, Kreyol evolved its own literature and poetry. Its status as an official language is due to the work of Haitians such as writer and poet Felix Morriseau-Leroy, known as "Moriso." He believed the language of the people deserved appreciation. Moriso made a choice to write in Kreyol at a time when French was the only official language. His poems expressed his love for his country and its language. Moriso also pushed to have Kreyol officially recognized and used in schools. It became an official national language, along with French, in the 1987 Haitian Constitution—183 years after the country was founded.

Haitian-American author Edwidge Danticat was born in Port-au-Prince and is part of the Haitian diaspora. She has won many international awards for her writing. Her young adult book, *Behind the Mountains,* tells the story of a girl's journey from her mountain village in Haiti to Brooklyn, New York.

Lyonel Trouillot is a Haitian writer, journalist, and professor of Kreyol and French literature. He has won many awards for his work.

Frankétienne is a Haitian writer, artist, playwright, and teacher who was nominated for a Nobel Prize in Literature in 2009. He was named a UNESCO Artist for Peace in 2010.

Music and Celebrations!

Food and music are important ways of celebrating events. They bring Haitians together—and who doesn't love a party? Haitians start the year off with a bang on January 1, with the combined holiday of New Year's Day and Independence Day. The day is marked with parades in the capital, as well as fireworks and concerts. Joumou is traditionally eaten on Independence Day as a celebration of freedom. It is a thick, pumpkin soup with beef, peppers, and sometimes noodles. The soup has history. Enslaved peoples were not allowed to eat it as it was considered too good for them. So, it is now seen as a "freedom soup." Independence Day is followed by Ancestry Day on January 7, and several weeks later by Kanaval. Kanaval in Port-au-Prince is a massive pre-Easter celebration that ends on Mardi Gras, or Fat Tuesday.

Wyclef Jean, a hip hop and rap artist, is one of the most famous Haitian musicians. He immigrated to the United States as a child. He formed the Grammy-winning group "The Fugees" with fellow Haitian American Pras Michel and American Lauren Hill.

Kreyol Muzik is a big part of celebrations such as Kanaval. Haiti's music scene is vibrant. It reflects the country's geography and history. There are many musical styles that developed in Haiti and spread to the rest of the world. They include a Kanaval and dance music called kompa or compas, Haitian folk and vodou influenced mizik rasin, and a Haitian hip hop style called rap Kreyol. Most Haitian music draws on African rhythms and South American and Caribbean styles and melodies.

Kanaval involves colorful parades with music, dancing, and elaborate costumes.

Rara is a style of festival music of Haiti. It features bamboo trumpets called vaksens and different drums and percussion instruments.

Foods

All celebrations include special foods, but in everyday life, many Haitians eat foods that are common in the regions they live. The cornmeal dish mayi moulin is a staple. It is similar to grits or polenta and made with vegetables such as tomatoes, onion, pepper, and spinach. It is sometimes served with fish such as smoked herring. Haitians enjoy a salad or a side of alligator pear, or avocado, with it. Pikliz is served as a side dish for many meals. Like it sounds, it is a pickle of vinegar, cabbage, carrots, onions, and hot peppers. It is often eaten with giot, the fried pork some consider a national dish.

Tasso is a goat meat dish that takes several days to prepare. Cooks must soak the meat in white vinegar, then marinate in citrus fruits before cooking.

Closer Look

Haitian-Made Religion

Vodou is a religion and a way of life that developed in Haiti from the religious traditions of people from West and Central Africa. Over time, it was infused with the beliefs and traditions of the Catholic religion. Vodouisants, or people who follow Vodou, believe in one God, called *Bondye*. They also believe in spirits, called *lwa*. They often refer to their religion as "serving the spirits." Lwa can be called on during religious ceremonies, where they speak through people. Vodouisants meet in temples called *ounfos*. There, *houngans* and *manbos*—priests and priestesses—perform rituals and ceremonies. Vodou is a powerful force in the life of many Haitians. It reinforces their connections to family, the land, and the belief that people can communicate directly with spirits and through them. Throughout Haiti's history, Christian religions and the Haitian government have seen Vodou as a threat to power. However, Vodouisants often follow different Christian faiths as well. Haitian governments also tried to ban Vodou practices through a number of laws passed from 1835 to 1987. The laws were hard to enforce, though, and many served to reinforce misconceptions about the religion.

Vodou ceremonies begin with drumming and prayers, and song. Voudisants often gather outdoors in nature. They wear white clothing as a symbol of purity.

CHAPTER 5

Looking to the Future

Every year, on January 2, Haitians celebrate Ancestry Day. They mark it by sharing meals with family. Some may light candles at family altars. These are little tables with photographs and memories of loved ones. It is a day of commemoration, to honor ancestors who died during the long struggle. The holiday is a reflection of how the people of Haiti never forget the sacrifices made to create their country.

Committed to Freedom

Haiti holds the status of the world's first Black republic founded by formerly enslaved people. The ancestors of today's Haitians threw off the shackles of colonial oppression through revolution. The world then punished them for it. Haitians today are still committed to that freedom. They have endured crushing **inequities** that have continued since independence.

Diri kole ak pwa, or rice and beans, *salad betrouj*, or beet salad (above), and *diri djon djon*, a delicacy made with Haitian black mushrooms, are traditionally eaten on Ancestry Day.

Freedom and independence are values important to Haitians. Their rich traditions and celebrations reflect these values.

Instability Hampers Growth

Haiti has struggled with corrupt and brutal governments that have contributed to making the country unsafe and unstable. This instability makes Haiti even more vulnerable to climate change and natural disasters such as earthquakes. Severe hurricanes damage homes and changing weather patterns destroy crops.

Political instability also impacts everything from stable housing to the country's ability to grow its own food and adequately feed its people. In the past, when Haitians have been threatened by violence and lack of opportunity, many chose to leave their homeland to find peace and work in other areas of the world. But the world has become more reluctant to accept refugees and migrants from many countries, including Haiti.

Haitians will continue to depend on the land for farming crops and other resources. It will be important to adapt farming practices and resource use so that they are sustainable.

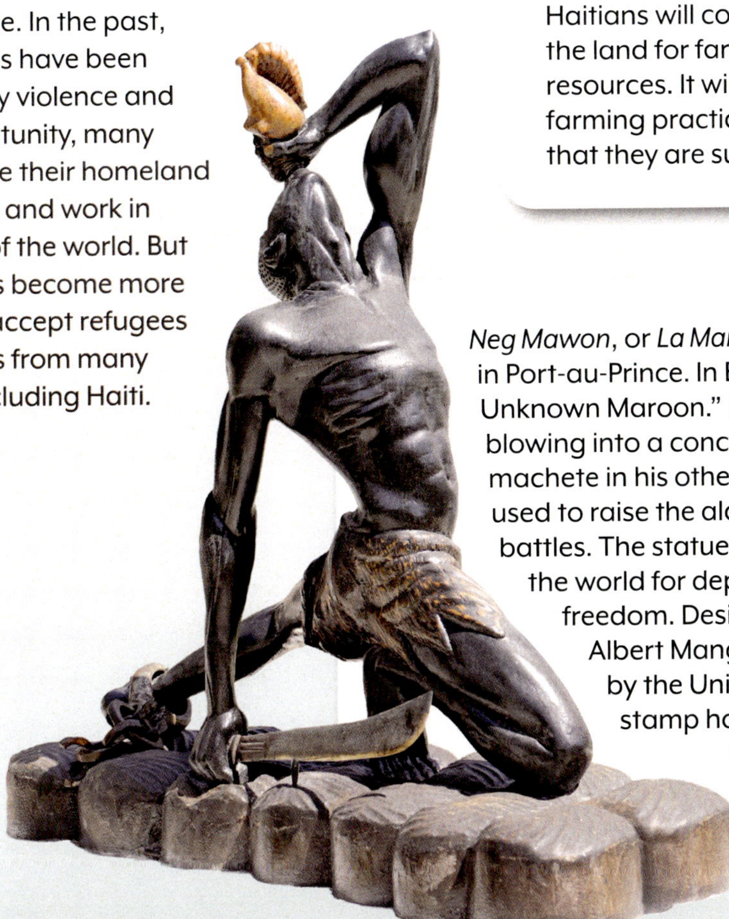

Neg Mawon, or *La Marron Inconnu*, is a statue in Port-au-Prince. In English, it is called "the Unknown Maroon." It depicts a Maroon blowing into a conch shell. He holds a machete in his other hand. Conch shells were used to raise the alarm during attacks and battles. The statue is famous throughout the world for depicting the struggle for freedom. Designed by Haitian architect Albert Mangones, its image was used by the United Nations on a postage stamp honoring the Universal Declaration of Human Rights.

Searching for Refuge

Unable to legally settle in wealthier countries, many Haitians migrated to South America after the 2010 earthquake. They worked in countries such as Chile and Brazil. Like generations before them, they sent money back to their families in Haiti. In late 2021, thousands of Haitian migrants were forced to flee South American countries due to the effects of the COVID-19 pandemic and other instabilities. They gathered at the U.S. border and crossed into South Texas. Most were deported, or sent back to Haiti.

In 2021, another major earthquake and the assassination of Haiti's president prompted the U.S. government to grant temporary protections to thousands of Haitians already living illegally in the U.S. The U.S. felt the conditions in Haiti were too uncertain to force people to return. But the migrations of its people are not a permanent solution for Haiti.

Haitians Leading the Way

Haiti's future depends a lot on its ability to establish and continue traditions of good government. Enormous debt has harmed Haiti's growth, however. It has made maintaining a stable government difficult. Haiti is rich in culture. Its artists, activists, scholars, writers, and ordinary workers have led the way in trying to build a more equitable country. The Haitian diaspora has brought many Haitians to countries all over the world. There, they work, set up businesses, and educate their children in a new land. They also support their families in Haiti and the economy of their homeland. Haitians still rely on each other, as they always have.

Foreign aid is an industry in Haiti, but it is often unclear who benefits the most from it—Haitians or aid organizations. Often, aid is directed towards programs that outsiders believe are important. Research shows that allowing Haitian communities to have more of a say in how money is spent leads to more success.

Closer Look

Reparations: Paying Back

In 2003, Haiti marked the bicentennial of the death of Toussaint Louverture. The event was also marked by a request to France for compensation for the crushing indemnity it forced Haiti to pay, beginning in 1825. Many **economists** have pointed to the debt as a major cause of Haiti's poverty today. The payments, known as the "independence debt" came out of the pockets of the formerly enslaved and their descendants for six generations. Haitians were taxed to pay it. It shackled Haiti economically for more than two centuries, as the country was forced to borrow even greater sums from French banks to pay the debt plus interest.

France has repeatedly rejected calls for **reparations**, including Haiti's request. It said it has given Haiti millions in aid. Critics argue that this aid is made up of loans and charity. These are different and amount to much less than the billions in repayment. In 2010, a group of scholars, writers, and politicians from around the world also requested that France repay the independence debt. The repayments would recognize the enduring harm done and help ordinary Haitians. It would also improve the country's economy.

Haiti's first democratically elected president, Jean-Bertrand Aristide, requested that France repay Haiti for holding it ransom. It was the first time a former colony requested restitution from its colonizer—another first for Haiti.

atrocities Acts of cruelty or violence

boycotted Refused to trade or deal with a country

carbon A chemical element that forms one of the bases of living things. Carbon compounds such as carbon dioxide contribute to climate change.

class A system that ranks people according to wealth or social status

colonial Relating to a colony, or a country or area occupied by and under the control of another country

commercial Concerned with buying and selling

communes Towns or large neighborhoods within a larger city

compensate To give someone money in recognition of loss or suffering

constitution The basic laws and principles of a country on which law is founded

cultural artifacts Things created by humans that give information about the culture in which it was created

democratic A form of government in which people elect their leaders

diaspora A large group of people who settled away from their home country or traditional homeland

dictatorships Governments in which one person has absolute power

DNA The hereditary and identifying material in humans

ecological footprint A way to measure the impact of human activities on the environment

economists Experts in economies, or the production and consumption of goods

elites A small group of powerful people who own a larger share of wealth and have more power than others

empires Groups of countries and colonies under a single authority

epidemic The rapid spread of a disease within a population at a certain time

fault lines Cracks in Earth's crust along which earthquakes usually occur

fertile Able to produce crops

food insecurity Being without a reliable and affordable source of nutritious food

foreign aid Money or assistance given by one country to another, through loans, gifts, or grants

French Revolution A period of radical social change in France that began in 1787 and ended in 1799

gross domestic product The total value of goods and services produced in a country in one year

indemnity A sum of money paid in compensation, often forced on a country under threat or at the end of a war

Indigenous Native to a particular place. Indigenous people are the original inhabitants of a place.

indigo A blue dye made from the leaves of a plant historically grown on plantations using the labor of enslaved people

industrial park An area of land, usually on the outer edges of a city, set aside for industries and factories

inequities Injustices or unfairness

informal economy Jobs, workers, and industries that are not regulated by government

informal transport Unofficial transportation services often operated by people who are self-employed

ingenuity The quality of being inventive or original

interventions Interference by a country in another's affairs

Kreyol Also known as Haitian Creole, one of Haiti's two official languages

leeward Located on the side sheltered from the wind

malnutrition Lack of proper nutrition caused by not having enough to eat or the lack of the right things to eat

Maroon Africans who escaped enslavement in the Americas in the 1600s and 1700s, and their descendants

metropolitan The areas included in a large, heavily populated city

poverty line A measure of the minimum amount of money needed for a person's basic needs in a specific area

prejudice Biases or opinions about a person or group that are not based in fact

protectorate A state that is controlled and protected by another

public transport Buses, subways, or other methods of travel that are run by the government

reparations Compensation given for an abuse, injury, or rights violation

republic A form of government where the state is ruled by representatives of the people and not a monarch

revolution The overthrow of a government. A revolutionary is a person who works to overthrow a government.

smallholder Small pieces of agricultural land, often supporting a single family

Spanish Main The term used to describe the Spanish Empire on the mainland of the Americas during the colonial period

tectonic plates Massive pieces of rock that make up Earth's crust. The plates are constantly moving as they float on top of a molten layer of rock inside Earth.

trade winds Winds blowing towards the equator from the northeast

Western Hemisphere The part of Earth that is made up of North and South America

Books

Cherie, Cat "Kreyolicious." *Haiti History 101: The Definitive Guide to Haitian History*. Kreyolicious, 2017.

Derenoncourt Jr., Frantz. *Haiti: The First Black Republic*. Thoroughbred Books. 2016.

Vincent, Dana K. (editor). *Haiti On My Mind: Stories by Haitian-American Teens.* Youth Communication, New York Center, 2010.

Websites

https://thehaitianroundtable.org
The website of The Haitian Roundtable, a non-profit organization of Haitian-Americans that seeks to redefine the narrative about Haiti and Haitians.

https://haitiancreole.net/learn-creole-online/
Learn to speak Haitian Kreyol with the help of this free online website.

https://haiticulturalx.org
Learn about contemporary Haitian and Haitian diaspora art and culture through this portal and blog of an organization that promotes Haitian arts in Brooklyn, NY.

About the Author

Ellen Rodger is a writer with an interest in the politics, art, and music of resistance. Her favorite Haitian musicians are Emeline Michel and Bigga Haitian.